Francis Frith's

Around
Hereford

Photographic Memories

Francis Frith's

Around
Hereford

Dorothy Nicolle

First published in the United Kingdom in 2001 by
Frith Book Company Ltd

Paperback Edition 2001
ISBN 1-85937-175-2

Hardback Edition 2001
ISBN 1-85937-350-x

British Library Cataloguing in Publication Data

Francis Frith's Hereford
Dorothy Nicolle

Frith Book Company Ltd
Frith's Barn, Teffont,
Salisbury, Wiltshire SP3 5QP
Tel: +44 (0) 1722 716 376
Email: info@frithbook.co.uk
www.frithbook.co.uk

Printed and bound in Great Britain

Front Cover: High Town 1925 77337

Contents

Francis Frith: *Victorian Pioneer*

FRANCIS FRITH, Victorian founder of the world-famous photographic archive, was a complex and multi-talented man. A devout Quaker and a highly successful Victorian businessman, he was both philosophic by nature and pioneering in outlook.

By 1855 Francis Frith had already established a wholesale grocery business in Liverpool, and sold it for the astonishing sum of £200,000, which is the equivalent today of over £15,000,000. Now a multi-millionaire, he was able to indulge his passion for travel. As a child he had pored over travel books written by early explorers, and his fancy and imagination had been stirred by family holidays to the sublime mountain regions of Wales and Scotland. 'What a land of spirit-stirring and enriching scenes and places!' he had written. He was to return to these scenes of grandeur in later years to 'recapture the thousands of vivid and tender memories', but with a different purpose. Now in his thirties, and captivated by the new science of photography, Frith set out on a series of pioneering journeys to the Nile regions that occupied him from 1856 until 1860.

Intrigue and Adventure

He took with him on his travels a specially-designed wicker carriage that acted as both dark-room and sleeping chamber. These far-flung journeys were packed with intrigue and adventure. In his life story, written when he was sixty-three, Frith tells of being held captive by bandits, and of fighting 'an awful midnight battle to the very point of surrender with a deadly pack of hungry, wild dogs'. Sporting flowing Arab costume, Frith arrived at Akaba by camel seventy years before Lawrence, where he encountered 'desert princes and rival sheikhs, blazing with jewel-hilted swords'.

During these extraordinary adventures he was assiduously exploring the desert regions bordering the Nile and patiently recording the antiquities and peoples with his camera. He was the first photographer to venture beyond the sixth cataract. Africa was still the mysterious 'Dark Continent', and Stanley and Livingstone's historic meeting was a decade into the future. The conditions for picture taking confound belief. He laboured for hours in his wicker dark-room in the sweltering heat of the desert, while the volatile chemicals fizzed dangerously in their trays. Often he was forced to work in remote tombs and caves where conditions were cooler. Back in London he exhibited his photographs and was 'rapturously cheered' by members of the Royal Society. His reputation as a photographer was made overnight. An eminent modern historian has likened their impact on the population of the time to that on our own generation of the first photographs taken on the surface of the moon.

Venture of a Life-Time

Characteristically, Frith quickly spotted the opportunity to create a new business as a specialist publisher of photographs. He lived in an era of immense and sometimes violent change. For the poor in the early part of Victoria's reign work was a drudge and the hours long, and people had precious little free time to enjoy themselves. Most had no transport other than a cart or gig at their disposal, and had not travelled far beyond the boundaries of their own town or village. However,

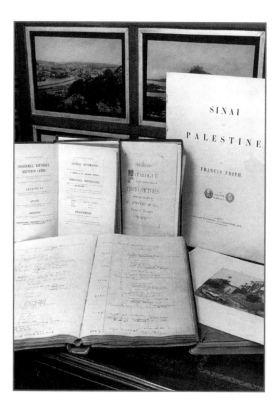

by the 1870s, the railways had threaded their way across the country, and Bank Holidays and half-day Saturdays had been made obligatory by Act of Parliament. All of a sudden the ordinary working man and his family were able to enjoy days out and see a little more of the world.

With characteristic business acumen, Francis Frith foresaw that these new tourists would enjoy having souvenirs to commemorate their days out. In 1860 he married Mary Ann Rosling and set out with the intention of photographing every city, town and village in Britain. For the next thirty years he travelled the country by train and by pony and trap, producing fine photographs of seaside resorts and beauty spots that were keenly bought by millions of Victorians. These prints were painstakingly pasted into family albums and pored over during the dark nights of winter, rekindling precious memories of summer excursions.

The Rise of Frith & Co

Frith's studio was soon supplying retail shops all over the country. To meet the demand he gathered about him a small team of photographers, and published the work of independent artist-photographers of the calibre of Roger Fenton and Francis Bedford. In order to gain some understanding of the scale of Frith's business one only has to look at the catalogue issued by Frith & Co in 1886: it runs to some 670 pages, listing not only many thousands of views of the British Isles but also many photographs of most European countries, and China, Japan, the USA and Canada – note the sample page shown above from the hand-written *Frith & Co* ledgers detailing pictures taken. By 1890 Frith had created the greatest specialist photographic publishing company in the world,

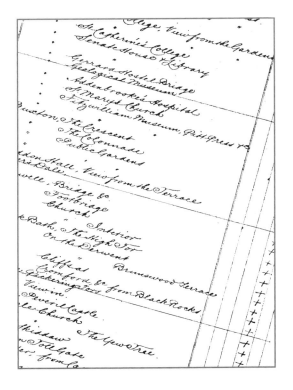

with over 2,000 outlets – more than the combined number that Boots and W H Smith have today! The picture on the right shows the *Frith & Co* display board at Ingleton in the Yorkshire Dales. Beautifully constructed with mahogany frame and gilt inserts, it could display up to a dozen local scenes.

Postcard Bonanza

The ever-popular holiday postcard we know today took many years to develop. In 1870 the Post Office issued the first plain cards, with a pre-printed stamp on one face. In 1894 they allowed other publishers' cards to be sent through the mail with an attached adhesive halfpenny stamp. Demand grew rapidly, and in 1895 a new size of postcard was permitted called the court card, but there was little room for illustration. In 1899, a year after

Frith's death, a new card measuring 5.5 x 3.5 inches became the standard format, but it was not until 1902 that the divided back came into being, with address and message on one face and a full-size illustration on the other. *Frith & Co* were in the vanguard of postcard development, and Frith's sons Eustace and Cyril continued their father's monumental task, expanding the number of views offered to the public and recording more and more places in Britain, as the coasts and countryside were opened up to mass travel.

Francis Frith died in 1898 at his villa in Cannes, his great project still growing. The archive he created continued in business for another seventy years. By 1970 it contained over a third of a million pictures of 7,000 cities, towns and villages. The massive photographic record Frith has left to us stands as a living monument to a special and very remarkable man.

Frith's Archive: *A Unique Legacy*

FRANCIS FRITH'S legacy to us today is of immense significance and value, for the magnificent archive of evocative photographs he created provides a unique record of change in 7,000 cities, towns and villages throughout Britain over a century and more. Frith and his fellow studio photographers revisited locations many times down the years to update their views, compiling for us an enthralling and colourful pageant of British life and character.

We tend to think of Frith's sepia views of Britain as nostalgic, for most of us use them to conjure up memories of places in our own lives with which we have family associations. It often makes us forget that to Francis Frith they were records of daily life as it was actually being lived in the cities, towns and villages of his day. The Victorian age was one of great and often bewildering change for ordinary people, and though the pictures evoke an impression of slower times, life was as busy and hectic as it is today.

We are fortunate that Frith was a photographer of the people, dedicated to recording the minutiae of everyday life. For it is this sheer wealth of visual data, the painstaking chronicle of changes in dress, transport, street layouts, buildings, housing, engineering and landscape that captivates us so much today. His remarkable images offer us a powerful link with the past and with the lives of our ancestors.

Today's Technology

Computers have now made it possible for Frith's many thousands of images to be accessed almost instantly. In the Frith archive today, each photograph is carefully 'digitised' then stored on a CD Rom. Frith archivists can locate a single photograph amongst thousands within seconds. Views can be catalogued and sorted under a variety of categories of place and content to the immediate benefit of researchers.

Inexpensive reference prints can be created for them at the touch of a mouse button, and a wide range of books and other printed materials assembled and published for a wider, more general readership - in the next twelve months over a hundred Frith local history titles will be published! The day-to-day workings of the archive are very different from how they were in Francis Frith's time: imagine the herculean task of sorting through eleven tons of glass negatives as Frith had to do to locate a particular sequence of pictures! Yet

See Frith at www. frithbook.co.uk

the archive still prides itself on maintaining the same high standards of excellence laid down by Francis Frith, including the painstaking cataloguing and indexing of every view.

It is curious to reflect on how the internet now allows researchers in America and elsewhere greater instant access to the archive than Frith himself ever enjoyed. Many thousands of individual views can be called up on screen within seconds on one of the Frith internet sites, enabling people living continents away to revisit the streets of their ancestral home town, or view places in Britain where they have enjoyed holidays. Many overseas researchers welcome the chance to view special theme selections, such as transport, sports, costume and ancient monuments.

We are certain that Francis Frith would have heartily approved of these modern developments in imaging techniques, for he himself was always working at the very limits of Victorian photographic technology.

The Value of the Archive Today

Because of the benefits brought by the computer, Frith's images are increasingly studied by social historians, by researchers into genealogy and ancestory, by architects, town planners, and by teachers and schoolchildren involved in local history projects.

In addition, the archive offers every one of us an opportunity to examine the places where we and our families have lived and worked down the years. Highly successful in Frith's own era, the archive is now, a century and more on, entering a new phase of popularity.

The Past in Tune with the Future

Historians consider the Francis Frith Collection to be of prime national importance. It is the only archive of its kind remaining in private ownership and has been valued at a million pounds. However, this figure is now rapidly increasing as digital technology enables more and more people around the world to enjoy its benefits.

Francis Frith's archive is now housed in an historic timber barn in the beautiful village of Teffont in Wiltshire. Its founder would not recognize the archive office as it is today. In place of the many thousands of dusty boxes containing glass plate negatives and an all-pervading odour of photographic chemicals, there are now ranks of computer screens. He would be amazed to watch his images travelling round the world at unimaginable speeds through network and internet lines.

The archive's future is both bright and exciting. Francis Frith, with his unshakeable belief in making photographs available to the greatest number of people, would undoubtedly approve of what is being done today with his lifetime's work. His photographs, depicting our shared past, are now bringing pleasure and enlightenment to millions around the world a century and more after his death.

Hereford - *An Introduction*

Hereford, the City of the Marches, has an atmosphere all its own. Although it has been a cathedral city for more than a thousand years, it is still today more like an overgrown village, with a charm and friendliness that is usually quite absent in our larger towns and cities. This charm is especially evident in the photographs taken by Francis Frith and his assistants a hundred years ago.

There has been a settlement in the area that we now know as Hereford for two thousand years – or quite possibly longer. We just cannot be sure. Certainly the Romans settled here, and built a small town – but not exactly where Hereford is today. Their settlement was a mile or two to the west, its position now marked by the village of Kenchester. The Romans called their town Magnis, but despite its name, it was not a particularly important town. It straddled a cross-roads, and was probably just one of a series of small towns serving the community around the Welsh hills.

Like many Roman towns throughout Britain, it did not long survive the departure of the Romans in the 5th century. When the first Saxons arrived in the area, they avoided this place full of ghosts, and preferred to establish a new settlement. They chose to live further downstream, sitting beside the River Wye, at a point where they could easily ford the river, and that is how the place got its name – Here–ford. These early Saxon settlers must have been quite a warlike group, because the first element of the name was a word in their language meaning 'army'. So Hereford means 'the ford where the army crosses', or 'the army's ford'. This old ford sits just below the site of Castle Green; we can assume, therefore, that it was here somewhere that the first Saxons settled, with at least a lookout point to provide them of warning of any attack. Presumably they were fighting for land for the families that arrived in their wake; they must have felt the need, once they had settled, to keep militarily alert in case the local Britons should rise up against them.

Before long the settlement grew, and some, at least, of these early pagan Saxons became converted to Christianity. These new Christians established a church, which very quickly became one of the main churches in all of England – a cathedral church. The town grew in stature; during the 8th century it became part of the most important kingdom in England at the time, Mercia, which was ruled by King Offa. On one occasion, in AD 794, King Offa visited the area accompanied by his wife and daughter, Alfthrytha, and they stayed at Sutton Walls just north of Hereford. While they were there, they received a visitor, King Ethelbert of East Anglia, who arrived as a suitor for Alfthrytha. But instead of being welcomed, King Ethelbert was brutally murdered; some say he was killed by the jealous wife of King Offa, but in all probability it was on the orders of Offa himself.

Ethelbert's body was decapitated and thrown in a ditch. And then the miracles began. A light shone out from the body so that it was found. It was put on a cart to be taken to Hereford for burial, but as the cart trundled along, Ethelbert's head fell off unnoticed. A blind man walking along the road tripped over it and miraculously had his sight restored. He picked up the head and took it to Hereford. Other miracles followed, and people visiting Ethelbert's tomb were cured of all manner of ills. Ethelbert quickly became venerated as a saint. His cult was to play an important part in the development of the cathedral here for the next four hundred years or so, drawing pilgrims from far and wide.

With the development of the cathedral, Hereford soon became the most important city in the central borders between England and Wales. In the centuries that followed, it was to see many armies crossing over its ford. In the reign of Edward the Confessor, the castle on the banks of the River Wye was attacked by the Welsh, and the cathedral church was burnt down and sacked. In retaliation, Harold Godwinson (later to be better known to history as the King Harold who was defeated at the Battle of Hastings) came here and rebuilt the castle before soundly defeating the Welsh.

Following the Norman conquest, Hereford's castle became one of a series all along the Marches (as this border region came to be known); these castles guarded the newly-conquered territories from those troublesome Welsh. The city was protected by the river to the south, but it needed the additional protection of a good, sturdy wall. This

was soon built; it enclosed an area that was considerably smaller than the city we know today. In fact, the northern wall followed a line just beyond the present-day West and East Streets. People coming to trade in Hereford quickly set up a market in an open area just outside the city walls. There may well have been an ulterior motive here. By trading outside the town, these people probably avoided paying the tolls that were due from traders once they were within the safety of the walls. An enormous revenue was probably lost as a result of this, and so it was not long before the city walls were extended to enclose the market area that we now know as High Town.

Throughout medieval times the city grew and thrived. It served a large area, and people would have come here from the central and southern Welsh hills to bring their produce for sale and to buy what they needed. They would also have been able to buy specialised goods that would have been brought up the River Wye from Gloucester and Bristol and from further afield - in fact, from all over Europe and the known world.

The world as it was envisioned in those days was a strange place, inhabited by many fantastic creatures and very strange people, even some with no heads but with eyes in their chests instead. At least, this was how it was drawn by Richard of Haldingham, a monk who came from Lincolnshire. His world was a flat world with Jerusalem at its centre; his depiction of it is known to us now as the Mappa Mundi, Hereford's greatest treasure. To our eyes it looks a very odd map indeed – the British Isles are strangely elongated. Incidentally, Africa on the map is labelled as Europe and vice versa! Despite its many errors, the map would have been an important source of knowledge; it would have been stored with early books in chests, some of which can still be seen in the Chained Library at the cathedral.

A cathedral was an important centre of learning in medieval times. Hereford, with its cathedral, its safe river crossing and its market, became a very important city as time passed. Today, sad to say, many of the old timber buildings of the wealthy merchants from those times have disappeared, but one remarkable building does survive. It is the Old House overlooking High Town, which was built in 1621 by John Abel, the King's Carpenter.

John Abel was given this title during the Civil War. At this time yet more armies came to Hereford, Parliamentarian armies to besiege the city, which supported King Charles I. During one siege, when Hereford was closed off from the outside world, John Abel built a mill to grind corn, and thus saved the local people from starvation. On another occasion the city was captured by trickery: the Parliamentarians pretended to abandon their siege, so that people opened their gates, only to find that the enemy had come back under cover of darkness. They then attacked, and successfully took the city.

That was the last time the city saw any actual

military activity, although in recent years a new army has taken permanent residence. Hereford is now the home base of the SAS (Special Air Service), an elite force that was formed during the Second World War to make raids behind enemy lines.

Most people visiting Hereford today are totally unaware of that connection. They see the city in much more benign terms – as a local centre of administration or for shopping. For some, Hereford is far more important as a centre of cider production: the world's leading cidermaker is a local company, HP Bulmers, which also has the largest container for alcoholic liquid anywhere in the world – it holds over 1½ million gallons!

But Hereford is much more than just a market town for people who like a drink. It is also a centre for the arts, and has been so for many years. It is one of the homes of the Three Choirs Festival (the others are Worcester and Gloucester). This festival ranks as one of the earliest regular music festivals to be held anywhere in the world, certainly the oldest in Europe. In fact, no-one knows when the festival actually started – there is an advertisement dated 1719 inviting people to attend the yearly music meeting, so it must have already been well-established even then.

Today the festival lasts a week and is held each August, with each city taking its turn once every three years. To begin with it was a two-day meeting; 'musick' was played both in the cathedral (when sacred music only was played) and in local halls in the city. It seems strange to us, but Handel's 'Messiah' was originally considered secular music. It was not until the Hereford meeting held in 1759, the year of Handel's death, that it was played in a cathedral for the first time. So many great people have been associated with the festival in Hereford, but perhaps the most famous of them was Edward Elgar. Although born in Worcestershire, Elgar lived in Hereford for some years; it was here that he conducted an orchestra for the last time in 1933 shortly before his death.

Hereford has been very aptly, I think, described as a village – 'a big village that sometimes looks like a city and speaks like a city and acts like a city'. Certainly, although Hereford is, technically at least, a city, it has never outgrown its origins as a market town serving a largely rural community. It has retained the friendliness and sense of community that is too often lacking in large towns and cities but can still be found in villages. The army's fording place has become a special place indeed.

By the River

View on the Wye 1892 29910
'How oft in spirit have I turned to thee, O sylvan Wye' wrote William Wordsworth in 1798. Some years later George Borrow was even more effusive. He described the River Wye as 'the most lovely river, probably, which the world can boast of'.

▼ **The Cathedral and the River 1910** 62500
It is possible to walk almost the length of the River Wye along the Wye Valley Walk. It is a walk of 112 miles starting in Hay-on-Wye (just over the border in Wales) and finishing at Chepstow, which is, again, in Wales. In fact, further downstream the river forms the border between England and Wales.

▼ **View from the Water Tower 1891** 29283
This is a view of Hereford looking eastwards, with the cathedral standing proudly above all the other buildings in the city. Today Hereford is rather more built up, but the cathedral still dominates the skyline, whatever direction you arrive from.

▲ **The Cathedral and Wye Bridge 1885** 4831
The ford that gave the city its name was probably a little downstream from here below the site of the castle. The first bridge on this site was built in around 1125, but this stone bridge replaced it in 1490. For the next 200 years it was the only bridge crossing the River Wye in all of Herefordshire.

◀ **The Cathedral and Wye Bridge 1890**

26957

Notice the landing stage with the boats nearby. Boating on the River Wye has always been popular, and the tradition continues to this day. Jerome K Jerome's book 'Three Men in a Boat to say nothing of the dog!' was published the year before this photograph was taken.

The Cathedral and Wye Bridge 1891
29263
Notice the way one of the arches under the bridge is totally different from the others. During the Civil War, the city was under siege; in 1645, the local people broke the bridge at this point to try and protect the city, but it was still eventually captured by the Parliamentarians.

▼ **Wye Bridge and the Cathedral 1938** 88427
A bridge is a focus for travellers. On the south bank there was originally a gatehouse which was demolished in 1782. Today, instead, a new complex, called the Left Bank, has recently opened on the site of Sully's Garage with a number of shops and restaurants overlooking the river.

▼ **The New Bridge and the River Wye c1966** H74075
The Wye Bridge was widened in 1826, but it still could not cope with the traffic. This new bridge was built in 1965 and opened in 1966; it now carries all the through traffic crossing the Wye from north to south. It should more correctly be called the Greyfriars Bridge.

▲ **The Cathedral and the Bishop's Palace c1869** 4833
This is easily the best position from which to view Hereford's cathedral, the Cathedral Church of St Mary the Virgin and St Ethelbert the King. The earliest stone church on this site dates from the 11th century, but there must have been a church here 400 years before that, because the first bishop was a man called Putta in AD676.

◄ **The Cathedral
and the Bishop's Palace
1891** 29266
The building to the left of
the cathedral is the Bishop's
Palace – it is considerably
grander than anything Putta
could have dreamt of.
Today's palace is very much
the work of Bishop Robert
Bennet in the 1600s. He is
known as the 'tennis-
playing bishop' – in those
days he probably played the
game we now know as real
tennis.

▼ **The Cathedral 1938** 88429

From all around the city the cathedral tower dominates the skyline. It sits on early 14th-century Norman foundations, which had to be strengthened in 1842. The views from the top are superb – but you have to climb 218 steps to get there.

▼ **The Suspension Bridge 1898** 41750A

Despite the different captions, this and picture No 41750B both show the same bridge. Perhaps more correctly called the Victoria Suspension Bridge, it is a footbridge, which was built in 1898 at a cost of £1,200 to commemorate Queen Victoria's Diamond Jubilee. Restoration of the bridge in 1967 cost £12,000 – inflation!

▲ **Victoria Bridge 1898**
41750B

The bridge links the city with the Bishop's Meadow and King George's Playing Fields; there are walks along the riverside here, with some lovely modern sculptures. Notice how the photographer has very carefully positioned the two boys. This was typical of the work of early Frith photographers - later photographers never seemed to take as much trouble.

◄ The Infirmary 1898

41769

The Infirmary, now known as the General Hospital, was established on this site in 1779. It cost £4,803 – well above expectations! In fact, it was a replacement: the earlier hospital was in Eign Street, and was later rented to All Saints Church as a workhouse.

The Castle

Castle Green Gardens 1906 56993
Across the Victoria Bridge, this garden still survives, although these days it is not so intensively planted. The original gardens here were planted out by Bishop Beauclerk in around 1745. He was the grandson of Charles II and Nell Gwynne. Nell was one of Hereford's most famous children, Charles II's 'Protestant whore', as she once famously described herself.

▼ The River from Castle Green 1938 88435

Notice the avenue of newly planted trees just across the river. These are now well established, altering the view here totally. Behind the trees are playing fields.

▼ The Cathedral from Castle Green 1891 29267

The Castle Green, to the east of the Cathedral, is the site of the old castle. It was one of the first 'Norman' castles in the country, although it was originally built in Saxon times, during the reign of Edward the Confessor. It is often forgotten that Edward was himself half Norman.

▲ Castle Green 1910
62505

This is Hereford's Nelson's Column. It was erected in 1809 to commemorate Nelson's recent victory at the Battle of Trafalgar. Lord Nelson had previously been given the Freedom of Hereford. Originally it had been planned that a statue should stand on the top of the column, but the money ran out, and the urn was put there instead.

◀ **Castle Green
Upper and Lower Walks
1906** 56992
One hundred years can
make a great deal of
difference to the plants. The
avenue of trees on the right
has since been replanted,
with the new trees
themselves now well
established. But today it is
the small yew-tree in the
middle of the picture that
now dominates this view!

Castle Green
Bowls 1910 62503
I like this picture of the gentlemen playing bowls on Castle Green. It is
typical of early Frith photographs with the people carefully positioned in
order to enhance the general view. As can be seen in the next picture, this
area has since become a more formal bowling green.

Castle Gardens c1960 H74071

Not only does the bowling green sit on the site of the former Hereford castle, but it possibly also sits on a very early monastery. St Guthlac's monastery was based somewhere here. It had probably been founded by King Ethelbald of Mercia in the 8th century, and may even be earlier.

Castle Pool 1892 29912

To its south, the castle was protected by the natural defences provided by the River Wye. Here, on the northern side, a moat had to be dug; it still exists, and still acts as a boundary between the castle gardens and the city just beyond.

Castle Green Lake 1910 62507 ▶
Despite the differing captions, this is the same
piece of water as in photograph No 29912, viewed
from the opposite direction.

▼ **Redcliffe Gardens c1965** H74073
We walk down from the old bailey (Castle
Green) to the site where the castle keep once
stood, but nothing that we see on this spot
would tell us that there was once a large castle
here. In recent years the waterway we see in
this photograph has been filled in, and the
whole site is now just grass.

The Cathedral

The Site of St Ethelbert's Well 1910 62508
This well is supposed to have originally sprung up at the place where St Ethelbert's body rested before it was interred in the cathedral. Unfortunately, the water from the well was linked into the mains some years ago, which stopped it from flowing here, so people can no longer place their pins in the water. Why pins? The tradition was that you placed a pin in the water and then used it to cure sores and ulcers. At least spring water would have been cleaner than river water.

▼ The Deanery 1898 41770

The Deanery, now protected by a much taller and thicker hedge, overlooks the cathedral close. Notice, if you look carefully, the small boy standing watching the photographer – he is just behind the tree on the far right.

▼ The Cathedral, East End 1891 29273

There is a particularly gruesome story about how the cathedral close was used in medieval times as a grazing area for pigs. Unfortunately the pigs started unearthing the bones of people who had been buried there, and so they were barred from entering – which caused a riot amongst the local people who lost their grazing rights!

▲ The Cathedral 1891 29269

It is interesting to compare this photograph with No 29268 – they both have the same date, 1891, and they are consecutively numbered. But look at the apex of the roof over the chancel – one of the pictures shows scaffolding where a cross should stand. It obviously needed to be repaired at the time, but our Frith photographer did not want scaffolding to appear in his postcard. Once he had chosen the image to be reproduced, he painted out the scaffolding so as not to spoil the view.

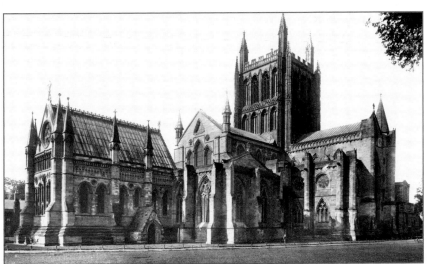

The Cathedral 1891

29268

Repairs to buildings like this are never-ending; there is now a semi-permanent masons' workshop set up here next to the church. It has proved difficult to match the new stone with the old, as there was not enough stone available at the original quarry nearby at Fownhope. The new stone is therefore being brought in from Matlock in Derbyshire.

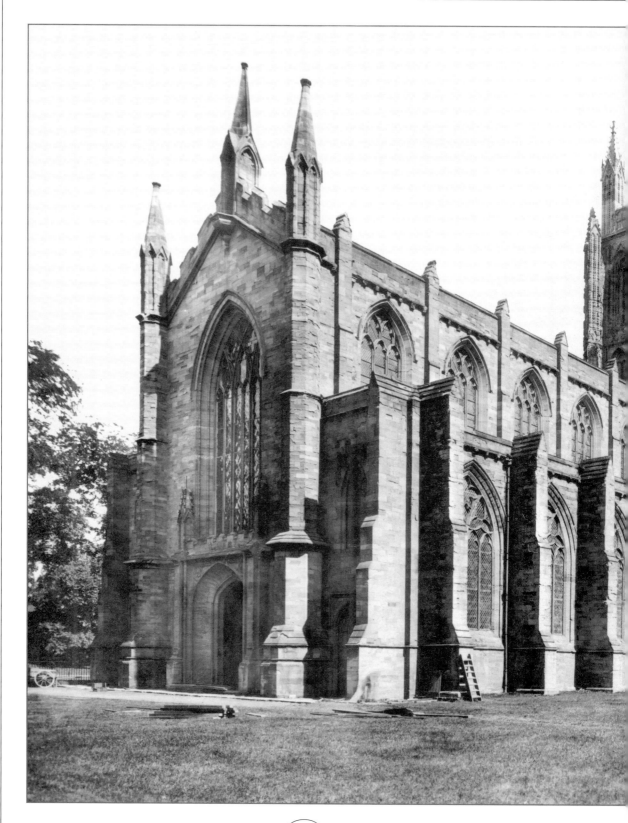

**The Cathedral
South West 1891**
29270
This view has
considerably altered of
late. The new chained
library with its
accompanying
exhibition has since
been built in the
foreground; it was
opened by the Queen
in 1996. Look
especially at the rather
under-stated west front
of the cathedral and
compare it with the
picture on the following
page.

The Cathedral, West Front c1910 51915A
The original medieval west front of the cathedral collapsed along with its tower on Easter Monday in 1786, bringing down much of the nave with it. Here we see the west front after it has been totally remodelled. The rebuilding was finished in 1908; the work had taken several years to complete. It cost a total of £15,550 16s 4d!

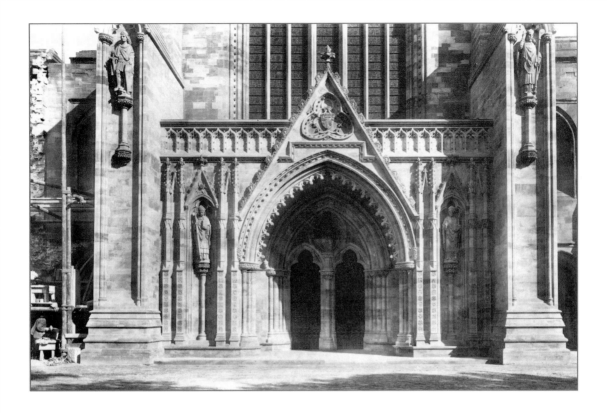

The Cathedral
West Door 1904 53001
The date on this picture is correct, however, as the central portion of the west front that we
see here was completed and dedicated in March 1904. The aisles and towers on either side
were then built and here we can see the scaffolding and a workman on the left –
work has obviously now commenced on the north aisle.

▼ **The Cathedral, North West c1869** 4836
The main entrance to the cathedral is normally through the 16th-century north porch. Notice the windows on the upper storey of the porch – this is a chapel dedicated to the Virgin Mary.

▼ **The Cathedral, The Screen and the Chancel c1861** 779B
We tend to take pictures of this superb quality for granted these days. But notice the date – 1861. To take this picture with the equipment he had available at the time, Frith could only use natural light; he therefore probably had to expose his glass plate for anything up to four minutes. The magnificent screen has since been removed.

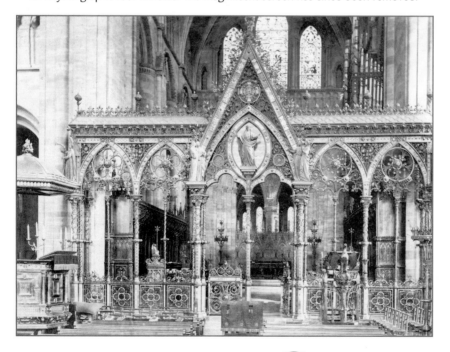

▲ **The Cathedral The Choir 1892** 29913
There is a lovely medieval tradition that still survives at Hereford - the inauguration on St Nicholas's Day of a Boy Bishop from then until the coming Christmas. St Nicholas is the patron saint of children, and his day is 6 December – he is better known to most of us as Santa Claus.

◄ **The Cathedral**
The Crypt and
the Chapel of Memory
1925 77353
At the time this photograph
was taken, the memorial
here was solely for those
killed in the First World War,
the 'war to end all wars' as it
was hoped at the time. The
altar is dedicated to St Anne,
patron saint of healing.

The Cathedral, The Nave 1891 29276
What a wonderful setting for a music festival. In 1726 a two-day Music Meeting was held in Hereford. It is thought that by that time these meetings had already become a regular tradition amongst the choirs of the cathedrals of Hereford, Worcester and Gloucester. Today, what started as an annual two-day meeting is now known as the Three Choirs Festival, one of the world's leading music festivals.

Extract from: The Cathedral, The Nave 1891 29276 **(on facing page)**

The Cathedral, The Font c1869 4849 ▲
This is probably the oldest object in the cathedral. The font must date from the 11th or 12th century; it would have been carved by master craftsmen working for what is now described as the Hereford school of carving. The carved figures represent the Apostles. One wonders how many babies have been baptised here over the centuries.

The Cathedral, The Font 1925 77348 ▶
When we see defaced carvings on churches we normally blame the soldiers of the Civil War, who did indeed cause a great deal of damage. In this case, however, the damage is thought to have been done during the Reformation period a century earlier. Notice the mosaic surround that has been added since picture No 4849 was taken.

The Cathedral, the Ladies' Arbour c1862 1166
The Ladies' Arbour is the name given to what remains of the old cloisters of the cathedral.
Today the cloisters are used to house the cathedral's shop and a tea-shop.

The Cathedral, The Chained Library 1925 77352
The chained library in Hereford's cathedral is the finest in the world, containing books and manuscripts that date back a thousand years and more. Not all the books are chained, however, chaining the books was an important form of security; it enabled people to read the books on the ledge below, while ensuring that they could not be taken away. Books were very precious indeed.

The Town

King Street and the Cathedral Tower 1891 29292
This view has totally changed today. The removal of the building at the end of the street has opened up the cathedral close just behind. Again, this is a beautifully-designed picture, with thought being given as to how the people are positioned, although they are quite naturally going about their business.

◀ **Broad Street c1965**
H74077
Some architectural
changes are unfortunate,
to say the least. Notice
how the four buildings
to the immediate right of
the Museum in the
previous picture have
now been replaced by
two modern office
blocks. Should it have
ever been allowed?

◀ Broad Street c1950

H74041

The very ornate building on the left is the city's Museum and Art Gallery, which dates from 1874. It was a gift by James Rankin to the Woolhope Naturalists Field Club as a home for their collections and a place for them to meet. Today the Club has a membership of around 1,000 people.

▼ Broad Street 1891

29284

The carriages are parked in the middle of the road while their drivers stand and gossip. Nearer to the foreground lie the droppings deposited earlier by the horses!

◀ Broad Street 1925

77341

Aren't the old cars parked in the street in this picture just wonderful! At the time this photograph was taken, Hereford was still holding an annual Hereford City Trophy, at which motor manufacturers put their cars on display (an early Motor Show, I suppose). The centre for the meeting was the Green Dragon Hotel, seen here on the left.

◀ **The Green Dragon Hotel c1965** H74067
This picture shows off the really beautiful wrought iron work on both sides of the road. Fortunately, this all still survives. So many other examples around the country have since been removed or were melted down for the war effort in the 1940s.

◀ **General View 1898**
41750
This is a view looking back down along Broad Street; it will have been taken from the tower of All Saints Church.

◀ **St Aubery Charity Houses, Berrington Street c1960** H74118
Aubery's Almshouses were founded by Mrs Mary Price in 1636. She endowed £200 (an enormous sum of money in those days) for the provision of cottages for 'poor widows and single women of good character'. She also stipulated that the women should be not less than 60 years old.

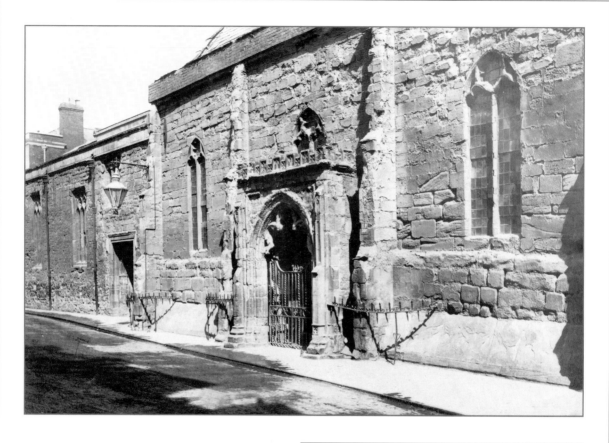

All Saints Church 1898 41763 ▲
All Saints Church looks in a very poor state of
repair. Recently it has been totally restored, both
inside and out. Although still a church, it also
houses a modern restaurant. This helps to fund
the church; it has been beautifully designed,
mixing the old with the new. Other churches
would be wise to look to All Saints for guidance!

All Saints Church ▶
The Pulpit 1898 41765
The modern restaurant is housed at the west end
of the nave, leaving the east end and chancel to
continue to perform their original purpose as a
place of worship. We tend to forget today that
many of our churches were originally used for a
dual purpose as both a meeting place
and a church.

◀ **All Saints Church, The Choir Stalls 1898** 41766
All Saints church still contains some fine furniture, such as these beautifully-carved choir stalls. The church also once had a large chained library of its own, but this collection is now kept with the other library at the cathedral.

▼ **Eign Gate c1950** H74038
In 1950, traffic was still using this road – but it was not to do so for long. It was the first street in Hereford to be pedestrianised. 'Eign' is a strange word – it is an old Saxon word meaning marshland, implying perhaps that the land near the river to the west of the town, to which this street leads, was very boggy.

Widemarsh Street c1950 H74032
David Garrick, England's greatest 18th-century
actor, was born in Hereford in 1717. He was
born in the Angel Inn, which can be seen in this
photograph, although here the building has
been renamed the Raven. Garrick was baptised
in All Saints Church, close by.

High Street c1950 H74039
This is the view looking in the opposite direction to photograph No
H74038. We see a number of familiar names here – although
Marks and Spencer (on the left) has since moved across the street.
Marchants, half-way down on the right, is said to be haunted by an
apothecary who committed suicide after he accidentally mixed a
medicine for a young boy and poisoned him.

High Town 1898 41751
In 1898 this was
obviously an important
trading area. Originally
just outside the town
walls, it probably started
as an open market area
where people came to
trade - they avoided
paying the tolls payable
within the town
boundaries. But even in
the 1200s, new town
walls stretched out
beyond this area and
enveloped it.

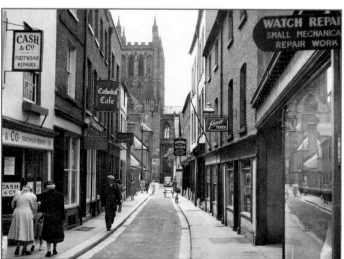

◀ **Church Street c1950** H74042
Linking High Town and the cathedral
is this narrow little lane, Church
Street. It was here that the cathedral
organist, G R Sinclair, lived. He was
a close friend of Sir Edward Elgar;
it was the sound of Sinclair's dog
playing in the river that inspired the
eleventh of Elgar's Enigma Variations.
Dan, the dog, is buried in the garden.

High Town 1925 77336

Note the changes in modes of transport compared with photograph No 41751 after a period of only 25 years! The horse-drawn carts (and omnibuses) have now been replaced by motor cars and bicycles. You would think a wide street like this could cope even with modern traffic, but in fact it has now been pedestrianised, with areas to sit and trees planted for shade.

▼ High Town c1950
H74034

There are some rather fine street signs in this photograph. At the far end is a Chemist & Optician warning 'Don't neglect your eyes' and advertising 'Qualified Optician here'.

High Town 1925 77337

Every year a May Fair takes over the centre of Hereford. It dates from 1121, when a charter was given by Henry I to Bishop Richard de Capella (who also built the first stone bridge over the river) granting him the right to hold a three-day fair. Through the centuries the fair was controlled by the church; it was an important source of income until the Hereford Corporation bought them out in 1838. Compensation was agreed, and so each year twelve and a half bushels of wheat are ceremoniously handed over by the City to the Cathedral.

High Town 1891 29287
Many such old ceremonies still survive. Perhaps it is just as well that
wife-selling here has now ceased! As recently as 1876, a young woman
was sold at the Hereford pig market for a shilling (5p). Cheaper than a
divorce and a wedding! Apparently, she and her new partner were very
happy. Not all such arrangements were so amicable.

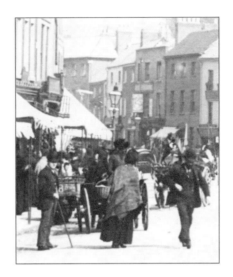

Extract From: High Town 1891 29287 (see facing page)

High Town 1891 29285
Notice the two ladies on
the left sheltering under
the umbrella and
dressed totally in black.
Mourning in Victorian
times was a very
serious and long-drawn-
out process, and
considerable investment
was put into it. Just on
the edge of the picture
to the right is a shop
describing itself as a
'Funeral and Family
Mourning House'.

High Town
The Old House 1925 77338
It is just possible to make out the word 'BANK' over
the windows on the left. At one time the building
was a branch of the Worcester City and County
Bank, which was later taken over by Lloyds Bank.
It was Lloyds that gave the building to the city in
1928; it was then converted into a museum.

The Old House 1898 41752

The Old House was built in 1621, the year after the Pilgrim Fathers sailed on the Mayflower. It was once one of a row of houses extending out into the middle of High Town. It was near here that Owen Tudor, grandfather of the future King Henry VII, was executed in 1461.

The Old House and High Town c1950 H74045

By the time this photograph was taken, the Old House had long been a museum; it still gives visitors a fascinating insight into how people lived in past centuries. There are some wonderful pieces of furniture: my favourite has to be a very old-fashioned version of a baby walker!

St Peter's Square c1950
H74030
St Peter's church, behind the war memorial, is the civic church of Hereford. It was founded by a Norman named Walter de Lacy, who owned vast estates locally in Herefordshire and Shropshire. He was a warrior lord controlling the Welsh Marches. He died in 1085 when he fell to his death while inspecting battlements.

◄ High Town 1891
29286
This part of Hereford was once known as Butcher Row, and in fact the first owner of the Old House is thought to have been a butcher. He must have been very successful in his trade – not only did he live in a particularly fine house, but he is also known to have paid 3 shillings (15 pence) in tax one year!

St Peter's Church 1898 ►
41768
We do not expect churches to change too much, but there are often changes in detail that we are not at first aware of. It is the chancel that is different here, with a single lancet window where once there were four. And the clock has been moved too.

The New Municipal Buildings 1904 51913 ►
The Town Hall (for some reason it has never been known as a 'City' Hall, despite Hereford's city status) in St Owen's Street has not changed at all in one hundred years. The charters for the city are all housed here; the oldest surviving charter dates from the reign of Richard I, and was issued by him in order to raise money to fund his Crusades. The Corporation of Hereford was found by government commissioners in the 1830s to be 'poor, but more honest than most', a description that delights me!

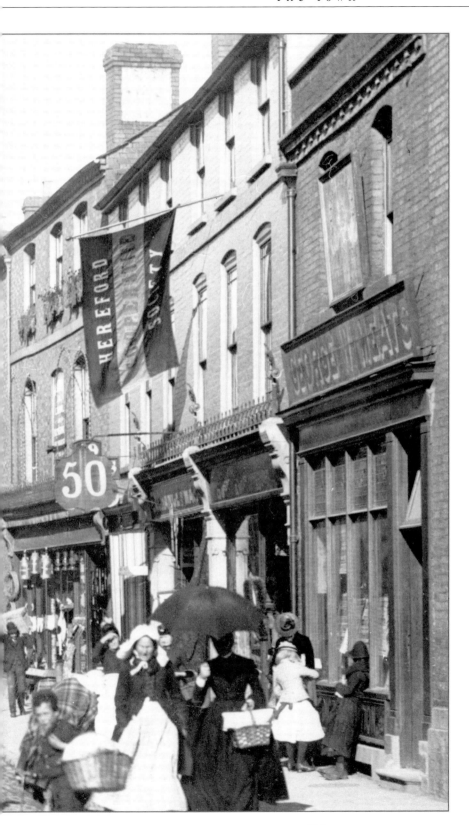

**Commercial Street
1891** 29288
This street has changed
so much that it is now
almost impossible to
recognise. But
something still survives
– that large kettle
hanging from the
building on the left is
still there. It hangs
outside the modern
Waterstones: it is
actually part of the
agreement of the lease
of the building that it
should continue to hang
there in the future.

The Kerry Arms Hotel and Commercial Road c1950 H74037
Despite its Irish-sounding name, this pub is named after John Kerry, who was once an innkeeper and Mayor in Hereford – way back in 1555!

◀ **Commercial Road
c1950** H74036
The lady walking
unconcernedly across
the road without looking
where she is going could
never do that today. This
cross-roads is now a
very busy junction
controlled by numerous
traffic lights and
pedestrian crossings.

◀ **Commercial Road
c1950** H74035
Commercial Road should
surely be renamed 'Fast
Food Street' these days.
There were always pubs
along here, but these are
now augmented with
countless takeaways
providing all types of
food – Indian, Chinese,
Italian, even one or two
English chippies.

◀ **The Coningsby Hospital c1950** H74010 Despite its name, this was never a hospital in the modern sense; it was a place of refuge providing hospitality, in this case for eleven 'worn out' soldiers and 'faithful' servants. It originated as part of the Blackfriars monastery, but it survived Henry VIII's dissolution of the monasteries and was taken over in 1617 by Sir Thomas Coningsby - hence its name.

◄ **The Training College 1904** 51914
At the time this photograph was taken, this building was used as a teacher training college. It has since become the Royal National College of the Blind, and was re-opened as such by Prince Charles in 1979.

**The Coningsby ►
Hospital, the
Courtyard c1960**
H74119
This refuge would have been well known to Nell Gwynn (orange seller, actress and mistress of Charles II) who came from Hereford. It is thought that she persuaded King Charles to establish a similar institution for retired solders in London – the now very well-known Chelsea Pensioners Hospital.

◄ **Blackfriars Monastery 1891**
29289
By the end of the 19th century, this was all that remained of the old Blackfriars Monastery. Modern conservators tend to clean up these sites so much that any romanticism is totally lost, even if the present-day rose garden looks beautiful in the summer. The first monastery was sited within the town, but it was moved here in 1322 by Bishop Cantilupe. In 1941 some ground here collapsed, revealing an underground passage leading towards the city; it is thought to have been dug as an escape route in case the city was attacked.

The Preaching Cross 1891 ▶
29290
It is an amazing fact that this is the only surviving friar's preaching cross left in England. The monastery here was built on land given by Sir John Daniel – he was later beheaded during the baronial wars in the reign of Edward III.

▼ The Livestock Market c1965 H74062
Originally, livestock markets were held in various streets in the city. That changed in 1856 when animal markets were all moved to one site to the north of the old city. By the 1960s, when this photograph was taken, Hereford's market was one of the busiest in the country, selling over 400,000 animals (cattle, sheep, pigs and horses) a year.

▲ Belmont Provisional Cathedral 1898 41753
What is a 'provisional' cathedral ? It was founded in the 19th century, becoming a 'provisional' cathedral in 1855; although the building was completed in 1882, it did not become a proper cathedral until 1916. However, it was a cathedral for only four years before becoming the abbey that it still is today.

◀ **Belmont Provisional Cathedral 1898** 41755
Belmont is a Benedictine monastery – the order was originally founded by St Benedict as long ago as 530 AD, so that it is the oldest of all the Christian monastic orders. Today there are still over 20 Benedictine monasteries to be found throughout the world.

Around Hereford
Travelling South

Grafton, General View 1901 47347A
The hamlet of Grafton is now almost a suburb of Hereford; it is really rather difficult to know just where this photograph was taken. Notice how what would otherwise have been a rather bland picture is lifted by the carefully-positioned man in the foreground.

▼ **Much Birch, The Church c1960** M182002

'Much' in a placename usually indicates that this is the larger of two settlements close together with the same name. The word itself comes from an Old English word meaning 'great', not that any of the villages in Herefordshire with this prefix could be described as 'great' these days.

▼ **Much Dewchurch, The Church of St David c1955** M183004

'Dewchurch' means Dewi's church, the Welsh form of David. We are here on the Welsh side of the River Wye, for all that we are in England. Despite this, the St David of this church is unlikely to be the David who is Wales' patron saint, but was probably an early local Celtic saint.

▲ **Much Dewchurch The Black Swan Annexe c1955** M183002
The sign tells us that this is an annexe to the lovely old pub which is a few hundred yards further along the street. Today it is the Charnwood Country Home for the Elderly.

◄ **Ewyas Harold, Main Road c1965** E181013
The settlements of Ewyas Harold and Abbey Dore sit in the beautiful Golden Valley. This name has come about because of a misunderstanding over the word 'dore'. It sounded like French 'd'or', so the French-speaking Norman settlers assumed it meant golden. In fact it comes from the Welsh 'dwr', which means water – hence the abbey by the water.

◄ **Abbey Dore**
Dore Abbey c1965
A1010
Dore Abbey was
originally a Cistercian
monastery; it was
dissolved by Henry VIII.
Much of it was then
dismantled, but some of
it survived; it was
restored a century later,
when the tower in the
middle was added. This
now houses the bells,
which ring out 'Be good
to thc poor, say the bells
of Abbeydore'.

Ewyas Harold
Temple Bar Inn c1965
E181017
This photograph is deceptive – the main street is actually at right angles to the camera, directly in front of the inn. The small ivy plant on the right now covers most of the building!

Abbey Dore ▶
The Church, The
Ambulatory 1898
41762
For a small village, this church is enormous. It was once two or three times the size. Today the entire church consists of what was originally just the choir and chancel, and it is still enormous.

Kilpeck, The Church, The Norman Door 1898 41773 ▶

Kilpeck church is one of Herefordshire's miracles. It is a miracle that such old carving should not have been defaced in subsequent centuries; it is even more of a miracle that it should have survived natural weathering. Actually, this doorway did have a porch to protect it, which was removed in the 19th century. In this photograph the superb detail of the carving can be clearly seen. Although Norman in date (the church was built in the early 1100s), the craftsmen who carved it would have been Anglo-Saxons, and the swirling lines of the dragons and birds are typical of their style.

Around Hereford

Travelling North

◄ **Hope under Dinmore, The Church c1955**
H264008
The church of St Mary's is the resting place of several members of the Conyngsby family, who owned nearby Hampton Court. This was the same family that gave its name to the Coningsby Hospital in Hereford. One memorial in the church is particularly sad – it is for a baby who choked to death on a cherry stone in 1708.

▲ **Hope under Dinmore, Markham's Filling Station c1955**   H264004
The garage is still here – but considerably altered, needless to say. It is now an Esso garage. But notice how in this photograph different brands of petrol are being sold alongside each other, Shell, Esso and Texaco; the pumps are exactly the same except for their heads. You can still get tea here too – from the Little Chef next door.

▼ **Hope under Dinmore, The Fork Road c1955** H264005
The Fork Road is so-named because it is the junction to Hereford or Gloucester for
those coming from Shrewsbury. This is the view just before the road starts to climb
up the Dinmore Hill. The smaller building on the left is a former toll house; in front
is a lovely old AA box, once a very familiar sight throughout the country.

▼ **Hope under Dinmore, Arkwright's Almshouses c1960** H264011
Although the Coningsby family owned the estate in the 1500s and 1600s, it was
later bought by Richard Arkwright, the inventor of the Spinning Jenny. These
almshouses were built in the village by the Arkwright family. Notice the vegetables
growing in the foreground, and the man gardening on the right.

▲ **Weobley, Kington Road
c1950** W304006
Entering Weobley today,
many people are taken
aback by this house. It is
not black and white; it is
black and pink! Actually,
this was quite a common
feature in the past – the
limewash which was used
to paint between the
beams was often dyed
with ox-blood, which gave
a strong pink colour.

◀ **Weobley, Elephant's Walk c1950** W304009
Address a letter to Elephant's Walk today, and no-one will know where to deliver it. The correct name is Bell Square, but it was briefly nicknamed Elephant's Walk by the local people following the visit of a circus to the town some years ago.

Weobley, The Village c1950 W304059
Weobley was named 'National Village of the Year 1999', and its easy to see why – the black and white buildings are totally charming. Amazingly, the island in the middle of the road once had a number of buildings on it, but these were destroyed in a fire in 1943.

Weobley, The Ley c1960 W304132
This just has to be one of the most beautiful houses in the entire county. It dates from 1589, the year after the Spanish Armada attacked England; it has probably changed very little, in outward appearance at least, since that time.

Index

Frith Book Co Titles

www.frithbook.co.uk

The Frith Book Company publishes over 100 new titles each year. A selection of those currently available are listed below. For latest catalogue please contact Frith Book Co.

Town Books 96pp, 100 photos. County and Themed Books 128pp, 150 photos (unless specified). All titles hardback laminated case and jacket except those indicated pb (paperback)

Title	ISBN	Price	Title	ISBN	Price
Around Aylesbury (pb)	1-85937-227-9	£9.99	Down the Thames	1-85937-121-3	£14.99
Around Bakewell	1-85937-113-2	£12.99	Around Dublin	1-85937-058-6	£12.99
Around Barnstaple	1-85937-084-5	£12.99	Around Dublin (pb)	1-85937-	£9.99
Around Bath	1-85937-097-7	£12.99	East Anglia (pb)	1-85937-265-1	£9.99
Berkshire (pb)	1-85937-191-4	£9.99	East London	1-85937-080-2	£14.99
Around Blackpool	1-85937-049-7	£12.99	East Sussex	1-85937-130-2	£14.99
Around Bognor Regis	1-85937-055-1	£12.99	Around Eastbourne	1-85937-061-6	£12.99
Around Bournemouth	1-85937-067-5	£12.99	Edinburgh (pb)	1-85937-193-0	£8.99
Around Bradford (pb)	1-85937-204-x	£9.99	English Castles	1-85937-078-0	£14.99
Brighton (pb)	1-85937-192-2	£8.99	English Country Houses	1-85937-161-2	£17.99
British Life A Century Ago	1-85937-103-5	£17.99	Around Exeter	1-85937-126-4	£12.99
British Life A Century Ago (pb)	1-85937-213-9	£9.99	Exmoor	1-85937-132-9	£14.99
Buckinghamshire (pb)	1-85937-200-7	£9.99	Around Falmouth	1-85937-066-7	£12.99
Camberley (pb)	1-85937-222-8	£9.99	Folkestone	1-85937-124-8	£9.99
Around Cambridge	1-85937-092-6	£12.99	Gloucestershire	1-85937-102-7	£14.99
Cambridgeshire	1-85937-086-1	£14.99	Around Great Yarmouth	1-85937-085-3	£12.99
Canals and Waterways	1-85937-129-9	£17.99	Greater Manchester (pb)	1-85937-266-x	£9.99
Cardiff (pb)	1-85937-093-4	£9.99	Around Guildford	1-85937-117-5	£12.99
Carmarthenshire	1-85937-216-3	£14.99	Around Harrogate	1-85937-112-4	£12.99
Cheltenham (pb)	1-85937-095-0	£9.99	Hastings & Bexhill (pb)	1-85937-131-0	£9.99
Around Chester	1-85937-090-x	£12.99	Helston (pb)	1-85937-214-7	£9.99
Around Chichester	1-85937-089-6	£12.99	Herefordshire	1-85937-174-4	£14.99
Around Chichester (pb)	1-85937-228-7	£9.99	Around Horsham	1-85937-127-2	£12.99
Churches of Berkshire	1-85937-170-1	£17.99	Humberside	1-85937-215-5	£14.99
Churches of Dorset	1-85937-172-8	£17.99	Around Ipswich	1-85937-133-7	£12.99
Colchester (pb)	1-85937-188-4	£8.99	Ireland (pb)	1-85937-181-7	£9.99
Cornish Coast	1-85937-163-9	£14.99	Isle of Man	1-85937-065-9	£14.99
Cornwall	1-85937-054-3	£14.99	Isle of Wight	1-85937-114-0	£14.99
Cornwall (pb)	1-85937-229-5	£9.99	Kent (pb)	1-85937-189-2	£9.99
Cotswolds (pb)	1-85937-	£9.99	Kent Living Memories	1-85937-125-6	£14.99
County Durham	1-85937-123-x	£14.99	Lancaster, Morecombe & Heysham (pb)		
Cumbria	1-85937-101-9	£14.99		1-85937-233-3	£9.99
Dartmoor	1-85937-145-0	£14.99	Leeds (pb)	1-85937-202-3	£9.99
Derbyshire (pb)	1-85937-196-5	£9.99	Around Leicester	1-85937-073-x	£12.99
Devon	1-85937-052-7	£14.99	Leicestershire (pb)	1-85937-185-x	£9.99
Dorset	1-85937-075-6	£14.99	Around Lincoln	1-85937-111-6	£12.99
Dorset Coast	1-85937-062-4	£14.99	Lincolnshire	1-85937-135-3	£14.99
Dorset Living Memories	1-85937-210-4	£14.99	London (pb)	1-85937-183-3	£9.99
Down the Severn	1-85937-118-3	£14.99	Ludlow (pb)	1-85937-176-0	£9.99

Available from your local bookshop or from the publisher

Frith Book Co Titles (continued)

Around Maidstone	1-85937-056-x	£12.99	South Devon Living Memories	1-85937-168-x	£14.99
Manchester (pb)	1-85937-198-1	£9.99	Staffordshire (96pp)	1-85937-047-0	£12.99
Peterborough (pb)	1-85937-219-8	£9.99	Stone Circles & Ancient Monuments		
Piers	1-85937-237-6	£17.99		1-85937-143-4	£17.99
New Forest	1-85937-128-0	£14.99	Around Stratford upon Avon	1-85937-098-5	£12.99
Around Newark	1-85937-105-1	£12.99	Suffolk (pb)	1-85937-221-x	£9.99
Around Newquay	1-85937-140-x	£12.99	Surrey (pb)	1-85937-	
Norfolk (pb)	1-85937-195-7	£9.99	Sussex (pb)	1-85937-184-1	£9.99
North Devon Coast	1-85937-146-9	£14.99	Swansea (pb)	1-85937-167-1	£9.99
North Yorks	1-85937-236-8	£9.99	Tees Valley & Cleveland	1-85937-211-2	£14.99
Norwich (pb)	1-85937-194-9	£8.99	Thanet (pb)	1-85937-116-7	£9.99
Around Nottingham	1-85937-060-8	£12.99	Tiverton (pb)	1-85937-178-7	£9.99
Nottinghamshire (pb)	1-85937-187-6	£9.99	Around Torbay	1-85937-063-2	£12.99
Around Oxford	1-85937-096-9	£12.99	Around Truro	1-85937-147-7	£12.99
Peak District	1-85937-100-0	£14.99	Victorian & Edwardian Kent	1-85937-149-3	£14.99
Around Penzance	1-85937-069-1	£12.99	Victorian & Edwardian Maritime Album		
Around Plymouth	1-85937-119-1	£12.99		1-85937-144-2	£17.99
Norfolk Living Memories	1-85937-217-1	£14.99	Victorian and Edwardian Sussex		
North Yorks (pb)	1-85937-236-8	£9.99		1-85937-157-4	£14.99
Preston (pb)	1-85937-212-0	£9.99	Victorian & Edwardian Yorkshire	1-85937-154-x	£14.99
Reading (pb)	1-85937-238-4	£9.99	Victorian Seaside	1-85937-159-0	£17.99
Salisbury (pb)	1-85937-239-2	£9.99	Warwickshire (pb)	1-85937-203-1	£9.99
Around St Ives	1-85937-068-3	£12.99	West Midlands	1-85937-109-4	£14.99
Around Scarborough	1-85937-104-3	£12.99	West Sussex	1-85937-148-5	£14.99
Scotland (pb)	1-85937-182-5	£9.99	West Yorkshire (pb)	1-85937-201-5	£9.99
Around Sevenoaks and Tonbridge	1-85937-057-8	£12.99	Weymouth (pb)	1-85937-209-0	£9.99
Somerset	1-85937-153-1	£14.99	Wiltshire Living Memories	1-85937-245-7	£14.99
South Hams	1-85937-220-1	£14.99	Around Winchester	1-85937-139-6	£12.99
Around Southampton	1-85937-088-8	£12.99	Windmills & Watermills	1-85937-242-2	£17.99
Around Southport	1-85937-106-x	£12.99	Worcestershire	1-85937-152-3	£14.99
Around Shrewsbury	1-85937-110-8	£12.99	York (pb)	1-85937-199-x	£9.99
Shropshire	1-85937-083-7	£14.99	Yorkshire Living Memories	1-85937-166-3	£14.99
South Devon Coast	1-85937-107-8	£14.99			

Frith Book Co titles available 2001

Lake District (pb)	1-85937-275-9	£9.99	Luton (pb)	1-85937-235-x	£9.99
Sussex (pb)	1-85937-184-1	£9.99	Cheshire (pb)	1-85937-271-6	£9.99
Northumberland and Tyne & Wear (pb)			Peak District (pb)	1-85937-280-5	£9.99
	1-85937-281-3	£9.99	Dorset (pb)	1-85937-269-4	£9.99
Devon (pb)	1-85937-297-x	£9.99	Liverpool and Merseyside (pb)	1-85937-234-1	£9.99
Bedford (pb)	1-85937-205-8	£9.99	Surrey (pb)	1-85937-081-0	£9.99
Down the Thames (pb)	1-85937-278-3	£9.99	Buckinghamshire (pb)	1-85937-200-7	£9.99
Hereford (pb)	1-85937-175-2	£9.99	Heart of Lancashire (pb)	1-85937-197-3	£9.99
Brighton (pb)	1-85937-192-2	£9.99			

See Frith books on the internet www.frithbook.co.uk

FRITH PRODUCTS & SERVICES

Francis Frith would doubtless be pleased to know that the pioneering publishing venture he started in 1860 still continues today. A hundred and forty years later, The Francis Frith Collection continues in the same innovative tradition and is now one of the foremost publishers of vintage photographs in the world. Some of the current activities include:

Interior Decoration

Today Frith's photographs can be seen framed and as giant wall murals in thousands of pubs, restaurants, hotels, banks, retail stores and other public buildings throughout the country. In every case they enhance the unique local atmosphere of the places they depict and provide reminders of gentler days in an increasingly busy and frenetic world.

Product Promotions

Frith products are used by many major companies to promote the sales of their own products or to reinforce their own history and heritage. Frith promotions have been used by Hovis bread, Courage beers, Scots Porage Oats, Colman's mustard, Cadbury's foods, Mellow Birds coffee, Dunhill pipe tobacco, Guinness, and Bulmer's Cider.

Genealogy and Family History

As the interest in family history and roots grows world-wide, more and more people are turning to Frith's photographs of Great Britain for images of the towns, villages and streets where their ancestors lived; and, of course, photographs of the churches and chapels where their ancestors were christened, married and buried are an essential part of every genealogy tree and family album.

Frith Products

All Frith photographs are available Framed or just as Mounted Prints and Posters (size 23 x 16 inches). These may be ordered from the address below. From time to time other products - Address Books, Calendars, Table Mats, etc - are available.

The Internet

Already twenty thousand Frith photographs can be viewed and purchased on the internet. By the end of the year 2000 some 60,000 Frith photographs will be available on the internet. The number of sites is constantly expanding, each focussing on different products and services from the Collection.
The main Frith sites are listed below.
www.francisfrith.co.uk
www.frithbook.co.uk

See the complete list of Frith Books at:

www.frithbook.co.uk

This web site is regularly updated with the latest list of publications from the Frith Book Company. If you wish to buy books relating to another part of the country that your local bookshop does not stock, you may purchase on-line.

For further information, trade, or author enquiries please contact us at the address below:
The Francis Frith Collection, Frith's Barn, Teffont, Salisbury, Wiltshire, England SP3 5QP.
Tel: +44 (0)1722 716 376   Fax: +44 (0)1722 716 881   Email: uksales@francisfrith.co.uk

See Frith books on the internet www.frithbook.co.uk

TO RECEIVE YOUR FREE MOUNTED PRINT

Mounted Print
Overall size 14 x 11 inches

Cut out this Voucher and return it with your remittance for £1.50 to cover postage and handling, to UK addresses. For overseas addresses please include £4.00 post and handling. Choose any photograph included in this book. Your SEPIA print will be A4 in size, and mounted in a cream mount with burgundy rule lines, overall size 14 x 11 inches.

Order additional Mounted Prints at HALF PRICE (only £7.49 each*)

If there are further pictures you would like to order, possibly as gifts for friends and family, purchase them at half price (no additional postage and handling required).

Have your Mounted Prints framed*

For an additional £14.95 per print you can have your chosen Mounted Print framed in an elegant polished wood and gilt moulding, overall size 16 x 13 inches (no additional postage and handling required).

> *** IMPORTANT!**
> **These special prices are only available if ordered using the original voucher on this page (no copies permitted) and at the same time as your free Mounted Print, for delivery to the same address**

Frith Collectors' Guild

From time to time we publish a magazine of news and stories about Frith photographs and further special offers of Frith products. If you would like 12 months FREE membership, please return this form.

Send completed forms to:
The Francis Frith Collection, Frith's Barn, Teffont, Salisbury, Wiltshire SP3 5QP

Voucher for FREE and Reduced Price Frith Prints

Picture no.	Page number	Qty	Mounted @ £7.49	Framed + £14.95	Total Cost
		1	**Free of charge***	£	£
			£7.49	£	£
			£7.49	£	£
			£7.49	£	£
			£7.49	£	£
			£7.49	£	£

Please allow 28 days for delivery   *** Post & handling**   £1.50

Book Title . . . .   **Total Order Cost**   £

Please do not photocopy this voucher. Only the original is valid, so please cut it out and return it to us.

I enclose a cheque / postal order for £ . . . .
made payable to 'The Francis Frith Collection'
OR please debit my Mastercard / Visa / Switch / Amex card
(credit cards please on all overseas orders)

Number . . . .

Issue No(Switch only) . . . . .Valid from (Amex/Switch) . . . .

Expires . . . . Signature . . . .

Name Mr/Mrs/Ms . . . .

Address . . . .

. . . .

. . . . Postcode . . . .

Daytime Tel No . . . .   Valid to 31/12/02

The Francis Frith Collectors' Guild

Please enrol me as a member for 12 months free of charge.

Name Mr/Mrs/Ms . . . .

Address . . . .

. . . .

. . . . Postcode . . . .

Free Print - see overleaf